© John B

ME SANNIES ARE BRANNIES!

ISBN 978-0-9927460-0-1

Cover Design, Artwork & Drawings by Paul Dennis.
www.consul4design.co.uk

Published in 2013 by

LUVULL.COM
Publications

CONTENT

CHAPTER ONE

Introduction

Let me just start by giving the qualifications I have to write this. I wasn't born in Hull and I have never lived in Hull as such but I have spent my entire adult life living within ten miles of the city centre. I have worked, socialised, entertained people and been entertained in the city and have supported the football team since 1968. Yes I was at every match during the Great Escape! I am married to a Hull girl and have three children, all now adult, who went to school in Hull.

So I have listened to Hull people, talked to them and, by deed of pure interest, have taken notice of what they say and how they say it – the words they use and the pronunciations they employ. The whole thing has been and continues to be a source of interest and of fascination which has brought me an immense amount of pleasure and not a few laughs. There have been people who have thought I was patronising them when I have talked to them or questioned them about something they have said but, for the most part, people have been happy to indulge me. In the end talking to people about their dialect, their use and pronunciation of words has given me a whole lot of fun. I hope some of this has transmitted itself into the pages of this book.

This is by no means a complete work, nor is it 100% accurate. Whenever I have spoken on the subject or had excerpts printed, I have always asked for contributions, additions and corrections. Some words people tell me are "Hull" when they are used in many places; others I have quoted and apparently knowledgeable people have not heard of them. But I have tried and I have enjoyed myself trying so what I present to you is an appreciation, an interest and a love of the Hull dialect. Don't take it too seriously and please feel free to contact me with your feedback or your suggestions for changes. You can contact me via my website **www.johnbrien.co.uk**.

Many people assume (always a bad thing to do) that, as a large northern city, a large Yorkshire city in fact, Hull will be home to a stereotypical northern or Yorkshire accent or dialect. Wrong! People from Hull speak like no others – not like Leeds, Newcastle, Liverpool or any other big city north of Watford. All are individual but Hull is just that bit more special. And what's more nobody outside the area seems aware of it. Even a well known publisher of books on dialects was of the opinion that Hull doesn't have a distinctive dialect worthy of a book. People all over the place have a go at talking Geordie or Scouse – they say *Canny* and *Howay the Lads* or they stick their hands over their noses and try to impersonate Ringo reading Thomas the Tank Engine – but nobody attempts to speak "Hull". Why? Because the accent is impossible and nobody knows most of the words!

At some point in the proceedings, so it may as well be now, I must point out that, having read books, searched websites and, more importantly spoken with and listened to people from many parts of the country, from Cornwall to Northumberland and from the Home Counties to the Lake District, I am now convinced that very few words or phrases are actually unique to any particular area. I guess that, as people have moved about more and more this has and will continue to become increasingly the case. I do hope that this doesn't mean that accents and dialects are going to die out but I fear for them in the long term.

As I alluded to, I think that any book like this will constantly evolve and never be completely up to date. Like the language itself, dialects change over time and, of course, I am human so there will be things I have forgotten and, dare I say, things that I don't know. So this work is quite personal, maybe a bit quirky but please think of it as a tribute to the dialect that has enriched my life. OK that's got the Hull people off my back so let's get on with the book.

+++++

It was one day in late 1967 that the bombshell was dropped. My father had been called to his company's head office in London and arrived home with the news that he was to be promoted to the position of Assistant Branch Manager in Hull. I was fifteen years and three months or thereabouts and had spent all my life up until then on the south coast. Not just the south coast but, until I was nearly ten, with a beach actually at the bottom of the road and, from then on, with one that was actually sandy a mere few minutes bike ride away.

I'd only ever heard two people talk about Hull before. One was my geography teacher, so I knew it was, at the time, probably the biggest fishing port in the world and that it was in the rain shadow so the average annual rainfall for Hull was only a little over half of that of Bournemouth. The other was the wonderful Eddie Waring with his own particular pronunciation of the words Hull, Kingston, Rovers, early, bath, up and under. Also I had been to see Bournemouth play Hull City once but that was the sum of my acquaintance with this fine city.

Throughout my childhood my parents had attempted to instruct me as to how I should speak. Both in fact had had elocution lessons in their younger days; my mother, who was from Croydon, at school and my father, who came from the East End of London, because he was told to lose his cockney accent if he was to become an officer when he was called up for the war. My early, slightly refined Brighton speech had, unbeknown to me, evolved into a version of the slow Dorset drawl, though apparently grammatically pretty good, by my mid teens. It was only when I knew that I was leaving my school in what was then Hampshire that a couple of my friends confided in me that they thought I was quite well-spoken.

So it was on 6th May 1968, aged fifteen, that I made my way by train to Hull. There wasn't room for me in the family car so I got a train to Waterloo then the Hull Pullman from King's Cross. Sort of from the ridiculous to the sublime I suppose though quite interesting to note that British Rail (remember them?) had chosen to discontinue the Pullman train to "exclusive"

Bournemouth yet continue it, and for several more years, to "unfashionable" Hull.

We had been up to visit for a weekend but that had been almost entirely taken up house hunting so in reality this was my first time. It was certainly my first time alone and I had to walk from Paragon station to the Dorchester Hotel where we were staying. I made two stops on that walk up Beverley Road; one to look in the windows of the old Rediffusion building full of television screens with a little man sitting in front of them presumably adjusting things; the other in the old bowling alley next to the, even then closed, Stepney Station.

I had a difficult enough job understanding my new neighbours, friends, schoolmates, shopkeepers etc. for at least four reasons. Many of the vowels were new to me; I had been brought up both at home and at school never to miss out letters, in particular T and H; the locals spoke so much faster than I did; but more than anything it was the sheer number of words that were completely new to me.

It may be helpful at this relatively early point to have a look at what a dialect actually is. The word *dialect* describes a variant of a language, in our case English, in which the use of particular words, phrases, parts of speech and grammar are unique to or at least common to the background of the people who use it (usually the area in which they live or were brought up but occasionally their social status). Closely related to almost every dialect is a co-existent accent which describes the actual pronunciation of the words used. Hull is richly endowed in both. Its vowel sounds are in some cases unique and in others more typical of a large Northern English city. Its words and phrases, though, are as typically Hull as are those of the Geordies and Scousers in Newcastle and Liverpool and as many if not greater in number.

Some of the words or phrases I will describe are what I call Pure Hull, that is to say they are unique to Hull and help to define the dialect. There are some others which, though not unique, when combined with those that are and used in context are just as much Hull and deserve their mention. In some cases, just to add to the confusion, words are pronounced oddly not because of the accent but because of some innate "Hullness" and I have included these in the dialect parts of the book because that is what they really are.

So 40 years on I began to formulate the idea of this book. In the same year, 2008, I saw that the new Express Holiday Inn in Hull had published a guide to its guests to help them understand the local accent and dialect. Well may they need this too as I can still recall the time during my first week at Hessle High School when one of the girls said, "Me sannies are brannies!". I had not the slightest concept of what she was talking about but everybody else in the room understood fully that she had a new pair of shoes to be used in PE lessons.

I was told to pronounce Hessle as if it were spelt Ezl and to ignore the H in Hull too. I went to the fish and chip shop and was offered cutfish. What on earth is (or was as you don't see it nowadays) cutfish? Certainly the people in the chip shops didn't seem to know. It was just fish ...... that had been cut. OK so the biggest fishing port in the world doesn't offer me the choice of cod, haddock or plaice, just fish. Perhaps the dictionary definition of the word *dialect* should be amended to include a complete lack of taste buds, at least in late 1960s Hull. Remember there was a thing called Hull Brewery bitter then so my theory may stand proven. Not that I tasted that until after my eighteenth birthday.

I write all this just to prove that I have some Hull history and, though not a Hull person, I do have some credibility in producing this work. I also have developed a love of the city of Hull and, in particular, the unique way that the people speak.

My thanks are due to my friends and family, some of whom even now still mercilessly take the mickey out of my own mixed up accent. Their constant ribbing has merely served to deepen my interest in this fantastic forgotten dialect.

As I said, I can still recall the time during my first week at Hessle High School, sitting around the common room chatting when one of the girls said, "Me sannies are brannies!". *Whoa*, I thought. Well maybe not that exact exclamation but something stirred in my mind that is still rumbling away over forty years later. I haven't just come to a place that pronounces things wrongly – er sorry, differently - I've come to a place with a new language. Incidentally I haven't heard the word *branny* for something brand new for many years.

CHAPTER TWO
Accent

As I mentioned, there are a number of quite distinct vowel pronunciations in the Hull accent; four and a half to be precise. These are found nowhere else outside about a 12 mile radius of Hull City Centre (well, four of them are) and are frequently, in fact usually, ignored by books on English dialects, quite probably because the authors have never ventured to Hull and just lumped it in with other Yorkshire cities or maybe just not even thought of it. Of course one of the wonderful things that having Hull City in the Premiership did was to make people think of Hull for the first time.

I remember attending a meeting of the company set up to oversee the regeneration of the city which was addressed by a man from a firm of consultants. They had done a survey of a number of cities trying to find whether people had a positive or negative impression of each. They found that many people didn't actually have an impression of Hull at all; it just wasn't on their radar so to speak. But that is a different story.

CHAPTER THREE
The Mystery Vowels

So what are these four mystery vowels? We will start with what I call the non-vowel - like the *a* in ahead or about and which a Hull person will use as the vowel in a word like bus. It's not quite the "true" Yorkshire or generic Northern *booss*, which rhymes with cat. Well puss. It's almost like *bss*, like there isn't actually a vowel there at all. There are loads of examples of this non-vowel – hut, bun, cup etc. It's kind of possible to make the three versions of this *u* vowel sound, Northern, Southern and Hull because that's how distinct it is. Listen to the crowd singing at a football, or rugby league for that matter match on television, "We are 'ull, we are 'ull, we are 'ull"

You can do it aloud or whispering, in public or in private and you can feel the slightly different parts of your mouth where the sound comes from. Yes you can - and it is a great selling point for this book as, if you are standing in a bookshop reading it and have got this far, you probably won't be able to do it without embarrassing yourself so you will have to buy the book so you can do it outside or in the comfort of your home.

This sound in itself would make the Hull accent unusual if not unique but there are others.

One pronunciation which aggrevates many people is the Hull *I*. Seriously, it aggrevates Hull people themselves, never mind outsiders. I know Hull people who visibly cringe when they hear it spoken yet who use it themselves every day. It is pronounced a little similarly to *ar* in Received Pronunciation (RP) but you have to say it a little further back in your mouth than that and with your mouth a slightly more open so it's about a quarter of the way to being *a* as in apple but longer. Once you have mastered that you can try out the classic shop girls' line, spoken when asking you for £9.99. Yes, she will ask you for *narn nar'y narn* or more nearly *na'an naa'y naan* (remembering, of course, to leave out the letter T). Similar examples are *I've* or *five* which come out as *arv* and *farv*.

"Thar'll be narn nar'y narn please"

The third Hull vowel is the "ai" sound which by southern standards is a kind of elongated soft *e* as in bed. Try to pronounce the word *made* (or for that matter *maid*). Think of *Med* then try and elongate the vowel and you get the Hull pronunciation. The mouth stays in the exactly same place which is entirely different from where a southerner's is when pronouncing *made*. It's really good when someone says they are going to make a cake.

This sound manifests itself particularly in the Hull word for children, which is *bains*. Many citizens of this wonderful city of ours have developed the habit of referring to their offspring not by their names but as *the bain* or *the bains*. They'll use this sound twice when saying *I'm takin' the bain to the park*.

Perhaps the most famous of all the Hull vowels is the O of Home. I genuinely think that *home* is the most difficult word to try and say in a Hull accent if, like me, you haven't got one. Home is the most difficult but there are lots of words that share the vowel. It is almost *er* but with just a touch of a nasal *o* in there. The winter of 2009/10 brought with it an excuse for Hull folk to use this vowel over and over again as, not only was there snow a-plenty but there was Snow on Frome Road. (We'll see later on that Frome Road is named after the River Frome in Dorset which is pronounced to rhyme with room everywhere else but rhymes with home in Hull). If you haven't got a Hull accent, try saying out loud *There's sner on Frerm Rerd*. If you have the accent then ignore this attempt at phonetics and say *There's snow on Frome Road* your way.

I said there were four and a half vowels unique to Hull so I'll have to justify that. The half is because it is similar to, though not as extreme as one used in another of England's great port cities, Liverpool. I'm talking of where the *er* sound as in bird is given a hint of a sound like *air*. This way you can get a circle pronounced as if it was spelt *sairkull*

This is most prominent in the nickname given to one of Hull's two famous rugby league teams. Hull or Hull FC are often known as the *Airlie Birds* after Airlie Street, a road adjacent to their old ground, the Boulevard. The play on the word *early* is obvious, almost ironic under the circumstances but the word early is pronounced that way by a significant number of Hull people.

That's about all I'm going to write about the accent. It will be helpful to use two bookmarks so you can come back to this chapter and bear it in mind when reading the rest of the book and try and pronounce the words I describe using the rules above. Well, to quote Captain Jack Sparrow, who may just have sailed into Hull in the Black Pearl, "Not so much rules as guidelines".

CHAPTER FOUR

Consonants

So much for vowels then, we'll progress to consonants. Generally speaking, Hull people are quite good at consonants, except when they are pronouncing the word consonant which often has an extra *T*. Frequently, though, *T*s and *H*s are dropped, though the letter *H* is often pronounced with a leading – er – *H* as in *haitch*. There's nothing unique about this of course but that doesn't stop us having some fun. I quoted *Ezl* and *'ull* earlier on and a nice warm summer's day or a particularly strong Vindaloo might both be described as *'O'* but we must take a little look at the frequent lack of the letter *h*.

One of my earliest memories as a teenager starting work in the city of Hull was of a salesman who came into the office once a week to telephone his regular customers. It took me some time to realise that he was not being rude when he used to say to one of them, *"ello you"*. Of course he meant *Hello Hugh*.

Similarly the names Helen and Ellen and Anna and Hannah are always muddled up; presumably the same people are delighted to see an *ejog* in their garden.

CHAPTER FIVE
Misuse of English

BBC Radio Humberside has from time to time broadcast a feature called the Grammar Police in which listeners (and, yes I was one of them!) would send in examples of use of the English language which were grammatically incorrect. A lot of these were genuinely poor and indicative of a lack of education or a "couldn't care" attitude but in many cases it was dialect. For this reason although *Misuse of English* might be a good description, it might perhaps better be defined as *Alternative Use of English*. Having said that, I have often stated, in serious moments, that if you use correct English, you will never be ambiguous.

This Misuse of English is equally abundant in both written and spoken form. Examples of incorrect English are there for all to see on notices, leaflets and in shops all over the city. Many are simple spelling mistakes, for which there is a fairly strong argument that the people should know better. I have a thing about sign writers and advertising agents; if you make a living writing the language then surely you should be proficient and accurate in your use of it. This sign on a well-known pub to the west of the City centre is not dialect, it's sheer ignorance.

CHRISTMAS FAYRE

2 COURSES £7.99

Now we get this as a well known chain of pub/restaurants has this on display outside several of its establishments.

FAYRE'S FARE

OK. Fare is a menu, a tariff a Bill of Fare to be more accurate. But a Fayre is a fete. A gala or similar.

We have one fairly common word which is used in Hull instead of another entirely correct word which is not used and, because of that, ambiguity is caused. Unless, of course, you understand the dialect. The word *while* is the Hull replacement for the standard English word *until*. *I'm away while Tuesday* or *I'm working nine while five*. Strange but you can cope with it in those situations. However, under normal circumstances *while* refers to something going on at the moment whereas *until* is about some event in the future so, in Hull, you get the ambiguity hence *Don't cross the road while you can see the green man*. It means *Don't cross until you can see the green* which to most people is the exact opposite. Perhaps we should ask the health and safety people what they think of teaching children not to cross the road while the green man is showing. Or do we get into a long involvement with the correct use of while as opposed to whilst? Confused? I am so you should be.

Whilst we are on the subject of misuse, sorry alternative use, of English, we must spare a thought for the humble apostrophe. Misuse of apostrophes is by no means unique to Hull; I have spotted errors in my travels all over the country. Apostrophes should be used to denote possession (*John's book*) or where a letter is missing (*It's* as a shortened version of *it is*). Under no circumstances is an apostrophe required when writing a plural. Yet how many fish and chip shops offer *patty's*? Even *pattys* is wrong as there is a fairly standard convention in written English that words which end in the letter *y* are converted to *ies* when there is more than one.

Then we have such lovelies as *potatoe's, sandwich's* (or *sandwiche's), chip's, fish's, pizza's, bus's* (or *buse's)*. I saw a sign at some roadworks whilst I was writing this stating *business's open as usual*. Top of the pile for apostrophes though has to go to a Hull one, the very best or worst use of apostrophes that I ever saw which was contained in a letter that I was asked to rewrite in the 1980s. It began *Dear Mr's Jone's*.

CHAPTER SIX
Verbs

I love the Hull dialect but there are two things that really get my personal proverbial goat. I refer to the use of *I aren't* and *you wasn't* instead of I'm not and you weren't. Of the two, I aren't is the more characteristic of Hull but both are common to the point of being normal.

Allegedly *I aren't* is a corruption of *I ain't* which is in common use in London, or was until relatively recently. *You wasn't* I have heard described as slovenly but it is so common that it cannot be just a few people's shortcomings; it must be dialect.

What is a little worrying is that both are taught in schools by locally-born teachers and it is in school that these two are most likely to be written, in an essay for example. Problems with dialect then? No, but possibly problems with marking. Can we be absolutely sure that people who mark GCSEs, SATs and the like will understand Hull has its own dialect and that the pupils sitting these exams will be writing in the manner that they were taught, or at least in the manner that they speak at home or with friends. They shouldn't lose marks just because they come from Hull.

We won't look too much at verbs, this isn't an English language lesson but there are two examples where the wrong one is used regularly. Both can probably be described by saying that the subject is muddled up with the object, by which people mean to say *can I do to you* but use the word for *can you do to me*. You have maybe guessed the two pairs of verbs that I refer to, they are *Learn and Teach* and *Borrow and Lend*. So we get *Can I lend a fiver?* which is intended to mean may I borrow a fiver but actually means almost the opposite. Then there is *Will you learn me to play the piano?* Well no, you can't learn anybody anything, learning is something you do yourself, with or without someone else's teaching. This also shows itself in the expression *That'll learn you* as said to the boy who fell off his bike when he rode too quickly. I have often been asked *Can I lend a pound?* to which my reply would always be something to the effect of *Certainly you can – who do you want to lend it to?*

One of the first Hull oddities that my family and I noticed back in 1968 was the use of present participle when we had been used to the infinitive of the verb. In many ways it is actually correct as it implies that something is occurring. The best example is that of our friendly shop assistant who will often say *Do you want servin?* My school taught me that she should say *Do you want to be served?* which is, of course, grammatically correct but over the years I have come to view that as somehow cumbersome. Some shop assistants even take it as far as *Are you wantin' servin'?* This is a grammatical mess but thinking about it logically the question is describing the customer's state. He or she is actively wanting something and what they want is for the shop assistant to be serving them.

Taking this verb use a little further is the lovely Hull expression meaning Do you want my help with anything? I refer to *Go'ow' ya won' doin'?* or if you prefer *Got owt you want doing?* That present participle just won't go away!

I even had an issue with a national company who provide out of school tutors to help children pass their exams. Their slogan, which was on all their cars at one point, at least in the Hull area but seems to have disappeared now (since its appearance on the Grammar Police I wonder) was *Does your child want tutoring?* This seems all haywire to me because, even if we replaced the present participle *tutoring* with *to be tutored*, it is highly unlikely that a child would actively want their services. So the question should be *Do you want your child to be tutored?* In the same category is the expression often heard at football matches which is unfortunately not unique to Hull but very common nonetheless, *The ref wants shooting.* It might be a good idea in somebody's opinion but I can pretty much guarantee that, however bad his performance and however well he may be aware of his shortcomings, he will not WANT to be shot.

Right, I'm going to end this bit on misuse of English with a reference to ladies' underwear. I had to fit one in somewhere so it might as well be here. I remember years ago a lady with whom I worked, who was in possession of both a really broad Hull accent and dialect, coming up with a wonderful but, in her mind, entirely logical alternative usage. She referred to a *Pair of bras* – well you get a pair of trousers and a pair of socks so why not?

"I'll take this pair please!"

CHAPTER SEVEN

Place Names and Proper Nouns

I'm going to look at place names now and I'm dividing it into two strands; one involves the mispronunciation of names which are proper nouns, the other is Hull's lovely trend to abbreviate or shorten place names. Several of the mispronunciations are street names, though the city of Derby is frequently pronounced Durby (the American way) when it should be Darby (as in Duane – this will be understood by Hull City supporters!). This would be entirely inexcusable except for the fact that the BBC's reporters so often refer to the town 40 or so miles South West of Hull as *Doncarster.*

"DARBY SCORES 6 GOALS!"

Duane Darby scored 6 goals in Hull City's record 8-4 FA Cup
win against the mighty – er – Whitby Town.

The names of shops or other high street establishments are often mispronounced and frequently it is back to our friend the plural. One name which many Hull people joke about is that of the well-known store Boyes. Correctly W. Boyes and Son, it is frequently referred to as *Boyziz.* I have heard the expression *I'm goin' on'road* meaning I am going along Hessle Road but sometimes specifically to mean I am going to Boyes. A lot of people jokingly refer to the Beverley branch as *Bow-yaze* or *Boy-aze.* What I haven't worked out is whether this is a case of Beverley people making out that they are posh or Hull people thinking or pretending that they are.

This plural manifests itself nationally with the use of Tesco's rather than Tesco – even the bus timetable used to show Tesco's until recently - but in Hull we have *Hammondsiz, Bootsiz* and *Marksiz*, or as I heard it called in Beverley during June 2009, *Marks and Sparksiz*. Asda, however is rarely referred to as Asda's in Hull whereas this is in common use in the south west of England. There is a firm of locksmiths in East Hull by the name of A.B. Rooms who are often called *Roomsiz* but perhaps the most bizarre of all though is Setam, a shop on Hessle Road, a name that was brought about by reversing the spelling of the word mates, a plural you will note, which is often referred to as *Setam's*. Is this the world's first double plural?

I'm taking my life into my hands when I say this but several street names are mispronounced. This has, I can only assume, come about because the people who use the names are unaware of their origin. Unless, of course, it was the people who actually built the streets and/or the houses there who were actually ignorant and their wrongly-given name has lingered on.

Like many towns & cities, Hull has its share of areas where the roads and streets are named using themes. Rivers (Longhill), engineers (Holderness Road opposite East Park), poets (also Holderness Road but west of East Park), battleships (Bilton Grange), composers (Anlaby Park Road North area), West Country towns (Bransholme) etc. It is because these roads are named after actual things, places or people that the mispronunciations stand out like a series of sore thumbs.

I list four roads for the sake of example

- Newcomen Street, which is named after Thomas Newcomen, the inventor of the atmospheric steam engine, which he designed primarily to pump water out of mines. How Hull could have done with some of these in the floods of 2007. They might have worked when the electric pumps of Yorkshire Water failed. However Mr Newcomen's name should be NEWkumman with the accent on the New. In Hull it is NewCOEmn street.

- Frome Road whose name is perhaps more famous as the one with the most "Hull" of all pronunciations. It should really be pronounced Froom after the river pronounced that way but spelt Frome which flows through Dorset and reaches the sea at Poole but no. Here it rhymes with that worst word of all in the Hull accent - *home*. Remember *there's snow on Frome Road.*

- Arundel Street is named after the town and castle in West Sussex, home of the Duke of Norfolk and, until recently, the traditional venue of the first match for touring international cricket teams. It should be pronounced A̱-run-dl but on Holderness Road it has become a-RUN-dl Street. Arundel, sometimes with 2 Ls, is also a fairly common surname in the area which, just to confuse the issue, is actually pronounced both ways in my experience.

- Holborn Street comes from Holborn in London which is pronounced Hoe-bn or Hoe-burn. The l is silent but off Witham it is Hole-born. A bit like a rabbit by the sound of it.

But what about Madeley Street? Is that named after anyone or anywhere in particular? It is pronounced *Madly* but I can find no trace of whether this is correct or not. I suppose it may just be the diametrical opposite of the BBC's pronunciation of *Doncarster.*

Then of course there is the strangely pronounced White-fra-gate, which is on the map as Whitefriargate and not a million miles from Blackfriargate which is pronounced pretty much as it is spelt.

One aspect of the street names in Hull that has caused amusement around the country is the rather quaint way that many, particularly older, people write their address. I suppose it may have been a way of directing people in general or postmen in particular. I refer to the practice of calling an address something like No1 A Street, B Street, C Street so someone might live in Chestnut Avenue, Buckingham Street, Holderness Road. Back in the days when he was a Radio 1 Disc Jockey, the broadcaster Noel Edmonds used to joke about this Hull phenomenon, often questioning how anyone could live on three streets. There are reasons for this, for example there are, or were before demolition of many of Hull's Victorian terraces, many examples of more than one with the same name. Hull possessed no less than nineteen called Ann's Place as well as three Ann's Terraces and two Ann's Courts so it could be an identifier. This view is further enhanced by the fact that some terraces had the same name as fairly major roads (though sometimes built before and sometimes after). For instance everybody in Hull knows Victoria Avenue which runs off Prince's Avenue but in the past there were five other Victoria Avenues which were small streets or terraces dotted about the city. Even so, Park Avenue, Cave Street would be sufficient but the Hull way of doing things adds Beverley Road to that address.

Whilst we are on the subject of roads, Hull is quite well known for having a series of roads radiating from the city centre rather like the spokes of a bicycle wheel. The most important are Hessle Road, Anlaby Road, Boothferry Road, which doesn't start until a couple of miles from the city centre, Beverley Road, Holderness Road and Hedon Road. The first five of these have a fascinating quirk in that at some given point, though it doesn't show it on any of the street nameboards etc., they become the High Road, i.e. Hessle High Road, Beverley High Road etc. Strange but engaging.

A different facet of the Hull dialect which manifests itself in the way people say the names of some places is the fascination with shortening names. This occurs with both road names and actual places so we have *Chants Ave* (which rhymes with ants) for Chanterlands Avenue, *Prinny Ave* for Prince's Avenue and *Cot Road* for Cottingham Road. Then there is *Vicky Dock* – people now live on Vicky Dock meaning the Victoria Dock Village, a housing estate built on the site of a closed and filled-in dock. Less politely (in fact to the disgust of some older members of society) I have several times heard Queen Victoria Square in the city centre, famous for its statue of the said queen above a set of public conveniences, referred to as *Vicky Bogs*.

Nearby towns do not escape the predilection for shortening names and residents can take a trip to *Brid* or *Cot* (Bridlington or Cottingham). The only question here is maybe why just a selected few places are treated in this way. I've heard *Bev Road* occasionally and a pub there has been interestingly renamed *The Bevvy* but never Bev for Beverley. Withernsea on the other hand is an enigma. No I don't mean why it was built in the first place, though you may wonder. Withernsea is both shortened and lengthened, depending upon circumstances. Although often just *With*, it is pronounced by a good many people with an extra syllable thrown in *With-er-en-sea*. The only other word I can think of like this is *um-ber-ella* which is also in frequent Hull usage even when it's not raining.

Combining the shortening of names with a dislike of change, aswell as one of the foibles of the accent, despite its relatively recent rebranding as North Point, the shopping centre in Bransholme will, I am sure, always be referred to as the Bransholme Centre or *Branny Senna*.

And while we're talking about names which get shortened or changed, businesses around the city don't get away scot free either. From my time working in industry I can remember companies whose names were shortened; Robert Sanderson Engineering, for example was always Bob Sandy.

I have not come across many shortened versions of Christian names that are unique to Hull, most of these seem to be nation or world-wide like Jim,

Bob or Kate but I have never seen the name Derek reduced to Des anywhere else though this is common in the area. Not a shortening but an intriguing pronunciation is that of the girl's name Doreen which is frequently D'reen. Incidentally this is one of those names that has completely died out - I wonder how old the youngest Doreen/D'reen is now.

People's jobs on the other hand, often come in for the shortening treatment. Some of these relate to the fishing industry which we'll see later but one job title which I always liked was the *Parky* for a park keeper. *Don't kick your ball over by the flowers or the Parky'll get you.*

C H A P T E R   E I G H T

Fishing

In view of Hull's history and its still being known as a fishing port many years after the demise of that industry thanks to Maggie and the Cod War (now there could be a name for a rock band – no I digress), it is pretty obvious that there would be some jargon from the fishing trade and this is true, in particular the names for the people who worked in it. Of course this is the case in virtually all industries across the country, if not the world but it is worth a mention, if only because anything that commits to words even the tiniest reference to the history of Hull cannot ignore the enormous effect that the fishing industry had on the development of the city. There are several books and internet sites that go into great detail about Hull's fishing heritage, all written by people with knowledge or experience that I do not have; I will therefore include a few paragraphs about some of the words used and move on. Bear in mind that Hull was actually only a great fishing port for about 90 years so all of these words came and went in that relatively short time. Who said English isn't an evolving language?

There were a few more general words or terms used in the Hull fishing industry that are worth mentioning. The containers that the fish was put into for selling were *kits* and the fish was weighed in stones. Perhaps most important is the fact that fish in Hull was never unloaded, it was *landed.*

Unloading is something that occurs in the other Hull docks with general cargo. In the same vein, the area known as the hold of a normal cargo ship was always the *fishroom* in a trawler.

As I said, the main thing that stands out to me is the selection of names given to the various jobs or to be more precise the people who did those jobs. Say "Fish dock" to many Hull people and they will very soon come up with the word *Bobbers*. This is the one word for a group of people that is known to be unique to Hull. These people have other names across the country, for example in Grimsby they are lumpers. The main part of the bobbers' job was to empty the fish rooms or holds of the trawlers as quickly as possible.

Some of the names are fairly obvious in their derivation but the word bobber has an interesting derivation. Or at least it has an interesting story told as to its history. Apparently in the mid nineteenth century, when trawlers were considerably smaller, the fishermen normally unloaded their own catch. However they knew they would make some decent money and wanted to get home, or to a local alehouse, or both, so they got into the habit of paying local people to do the unloading for them. They would pay them a shilling – a bob - to do this so the name bobbers came about. I do hope this is true.

There were of course many other jobs all over the fish dock that were essential to the smooth running of the landing, sorting, selling and distribution of the fish. There were *Belowmen* who worked in the fishroom itself sorting the fish into baskets of each type or species of fish. It occurs to me that these people could have been rendered unnecessary by the existence of *cutfish*. If fish shop owners and their customers didn't mind or know what fish they were frying or eating, what was the point of paying somebody to sort it all out? But of course there was a market well beyond the city boundaries where fish was sold and cooked by species. The Jamie Olivers of a previous generation would present each fish differently just as they do now.

Riggers were employed to attach wires to the trawlers to allow baskets of fish to be unloaded as quickly as possible. The *swinger* on the ship and the winchman (no special name there then) on the quayside swung the baskets over from ship to shore where they were caught by a *tipper* or *weigher-out* who emptied the fish into metal containers known as *kits* where it was weighed prior to auction. The kits were made to look as presentable as possible for sale by *dollarmen* and were then taken to the sales area by *barrowmen*.

Last but I assume not least were the quaintly named *fifthmen* whose job was to cover any of the team who needed a break but generally would help the team of *belowmen* who usually worked in teams of four, hence their name *fifthmen*.

Other people involved on the docks were *rulley men*. These were drivers of a kind of horse and cart, similar to a brewer's drey. The rulley was a common sight around Hull until well into the twentieth century carrying all sorts of goods from coal to fruit to packing cases across the city.

On the trawlers themselves there was a fairly standard crew, mostly with what might be called normal sailors' names for their positions. Obviously there would be the skipper (never the captain, always the skipper) then a mate, a chief and a second engineer etc. and a cook of course. There would be a number of deck hands depending upon the size of the ship but the expression that might have been put into the category of cuties was that given to the trainee. He was a *Deckie Learner*.

CHAPTER NINE

Hullness

As well as the dialect and accent, there is much about Hull that makes it stand out from other towns and cities. In 2011/12, a series of debates and a resulting exhibition took place, sponsored by ARC, the centre of excellence for the built environment (you can see why they shortened it to ARC) about what is Hullness. The geographers refer to the flatness, the fact that you can't see the rest of the city from where you stand at any point within the boundary (visitors sometimes call it "Big Sky City" for a similar reason). Compare this with hilly cities like Liverpool, Sheffield, Brighton or Newcastle. Well not if you haven't been there of course but, take my word, Hull's different. It affects the shape, the architecture maybe, the infrastructure definitely but the innate character of the place? I'm not so sure; that's got to come basically from human features. And the biggest human feature is the way the Hull people speak.

One trait of the people of Hull that does contribute to the character of the place is a deep inbuilt resistance to change or to any kind of new development. When I first moved to the area, the Hull Royal Infirmary had recently been opened. It is a tower block, typical of its time and it certainly has its critics from an architectural point of view but what a leap forward in hospital provision for the city it was in the late 1960s. But I heard so many people saying we don't need it or we've got a perfectly good hospital already. There was a hospital, yes, but it was Victorian, war-damaged, rat-infested and basically falling down.

More recently they didn't want The Deep, which is second only to The Eden Project as the most successful of all the Millennium projects; they didn't want the KC stadium, they didn't want the award-winning St. Stephen's shopping centre, they didn't want the new transport interchange. You get my drift.

They even argue about the name of the place. It is officially Kingston-upon-Hull but has always been known as Hull until some reason for an argument comes to the surface. The most recent was when the local regeneration people introduced a logo which was used when attending events to try and bring business to the city. This logo consisted of a cog accompanied by the word hull with a small h. Well all hell was let loose among the narrow minded who can't see beyond the tips of their noses. It was a logo – it wasn't renaming the city; it wasn't spelling it with a small *h*. It was meant to be eye-catching and it worked quite well ..... except for the people with Hull disease, the symptoms of which are a constant repetition of "we don't want that" whenever something new is suggested, brought about, built etc.

Of course up until fairly recently nobody knew where Hull was. Well not nobody obviously but very few would be accurate, though you could probably exclude sailors from that as Hull was, up to the latter part of the 20th century, a massive port. Although It was mainly a cargo port though there were passengers to several parts of the world, in particular northern Europe. You name it, though, and it was imported through one or other of the docks which used to sprawl along the banks of the Humber from the far east to the far west of the city and right through the city centre too. As well as all the cargoes which ranged from timber and pit props to food and perishables, there was a constant mixed cargo trade with Rotterdam and the Baltic ports.

The main export was probably coal from the Yorkshire mines, most of which went to various power stations and the like around the coast of Great Britain; this was the main reason for building at least two railways into Hull. Ironically coal is now one of the major imports. It's cheaper to bring it to the West Riding power stations from Poland or Argentina or wherever than from Castleford or Pontefract which seems odd.

Then there was the fish dock......

You could also include Germans in the list of people who knew very well where Hull is. It was never publicised during World War 2 but Hull took one of the biggest amounts of bombs of any UK city – far worse than many that brag how badly they were hit. For some reason Hull was never mentioned by the BBC or the press, it was always "a North East coast town" that was hit and rarely badly.

This thing about people not coming to Hull actually works in reverse too. I can't imagine there's a less-travelled group of people in the country than the population of Hull. Many have never been to London. I've heard all sorts of excuses from *I don't like the place* (they've never been so how do they know?) to *everything's too fast*. I've even heard people say they'd be scared of the underground. An awful lot of Hull people have never been to other parts of Yorkshire like Leeds or Sheffield. They've maybe been to *Brid* or *Witherensea*. Strangely, though, they can list out the bars down the main streets of several holiday resorts in Spain, Majorca, the Canaries or the Greek Islands. In some cases they could even name the waiters. Of course this is a massive generalisation; there are many Hull people who travel regularly at home and abroad but the number who don't and won't is striking.

So much of Hull's history can be shown to have influenced "Hullness" and probably a lot of this, in particular the international trade and all that brings with it, can take responsibility for the evolution of what are today's Hull dialect and accent and what, to me, is the most important thing that makes Hull what it is.

CHAPTER TEN
Drink Drink (Getränk Getränk)

Just to go off at a tangent for a moment, how many people remember the Hofbräuhaus on George Street? The supposedly German style bar with its "steins" of beer three quarters filled and left to stand / go flat / get warm until you ordered some at which time they just topped it up. Yes we all stood on the tables and sang silly German songs and drunk the tepid, flat beer like it was going out of fashion to music that was provided by what was euphemistically called an Oompah Band.

My point? I hear you ask. Well, it was the Hofbräuhaus, so why did so many people call it Hoffenbrowse? Another complete mispronunciation but quaintly Hull.

Back to shortenings for a moment; another night club was often referred to as Tiff's. Can you imagine all the hype and glamour surrounding Audrey Hepburn and **that** dress if she had been starring in *Breakfast at Tiff's*. It just doesn't have the same *je ne sais quoi* does it?

A number of pubs in the area have long been known by nicknames, often but not always derived from the name of a longstanding landlord or landlady. In recent years the pubs have actually been renamed to these. Examples include Parker's and Rayner's but if you go just outside the City boundary there is the intriguingly named Top House in Hessle. Probably the most famous is in Beverley where the renaming has not taken place but nobody refers to the White Horse. It is and will for ever remain *Nellie's*.

Now renamed Sharkey's the pub on George Street was previously the Georgian. Like a fine terraced house, you may think. Well no, you have to remember this is Hull and it was always pronounced like two boys names – George Ian.

I can't go without mentioning the Red Lion. Nothing strange about the way this pub is pronounced but it is unique. Known generally as the Red Lion Clarence Street, it is in fact the only pub in the country that is actually on four streets, being surrounded by roads. Who says this isn't educational?

CHAPTER ELEVEN
Rhyming Slang

Most people associate this with London, in particular the East End of the capital. In fact it is often referred to as Cockney Rhyming Slang and there is no doubt that this is where it has flourished the most. Surprisingly, however, its use in Hull is quite commonplace.

I cannot explain better than by quoting from The Book of Words by Tim Glynne-Jones:

> The beauty of rhyming slang is that the principle is so simple, anyone can make up new words. New expressions are added all the time. When the late Ayrton Senna rose to fame in motor racing, he at last gave the language a rhyme for a ten pound note (Ayrton Senna: tenner). Similarly in the 1960s the Irish singer Ruby Murray provided a handy rhyme for Britain's newly acquired favourite food, the curry. Her modern counterpart, Britney Spears, is now rhyming slang for beers. *If you've got a spare Ayrton we can go for a few Britneys followed by a Ruby.*

All three of these are in common use in Hull along with the wonderful *You're having a giraffe* (you're having a laugh) often pronounced with an exaggerated southern arr as in Gi-rarff.

I am certain that there are many more than this in use in and around Hull but I will list just a few hat have been said either to me or in my presence over the years.

Adam and Eve	believe	*Would you adam and eve it*
Borassic Lint	skint / broke	*Can I lend a fiver I'm borassic.*
Brown Bread	dead	*He's brown bread*
Nat King Cole	dole	*I'm on the Nat King Cole*
Pen and Ink	stink	*He don't arf pen and ink*
Tin Lids	kids	*I'm taking the tin lids to the park*

This last example of course is an alternative to the word *Bains* which we'll touch on later.

CHAPTER TWELVE
Cuties

I have called these "Cuties" as it is a summary of a few of those lovely little eccentricities of the Hull accent and /or dialect which don't really fall into any of my other categories.

One which hit home to me whilst I was still at school and I have loved every time I have heard it since is the use of the word *off* where the rest of the English-speaking world would probably use *going* or *going to*. This came to its high point in a cricket match that I played in when the captain called up one of the bowlers and said to him, "Are you off on?" It took me a few seconds to realise that what the captain meant was, "Would you like to bowl next?". The use of the two prepositions with opposite meanings, off and on, together like that is strange to say the least but I still smile to myself whenever I hear it. The use of *off* rather than *going* is actually quite widespread in Hull with such expressions as *Are you off shopping* and *I'm off to the theatre* in common use.

However the actual expression *Are you off on?* displays more than one peculiarity if that is the word. It also shows us another "cutie" which is the habit of asking a question when actually intending to give an instruction. What the cricket captain actually meant to say was *You are bowling next* or words to that effect rather than asking the bowler if he fancied the idea. The same use of a question can be heard every day in shops throughout the city, especially sandwich shops or takeaways. I refer to *Have you got a cheese sandwich?* or *Have you got fish and chips?* What is meant is *Please may I have a cheese sandwich* or, to use the local expression *Fish and chips twice please.* In many cases there is a pile of cheese sandwiches on the counter in front of them so they can see perfectly well that the shop has one. In other shops they make all the sandwiches to order in which case the customer knows that they haven't a cheese sandwich but will make one for them. It's just cute but have you noticed it is being supercede over the last couple of years by *Can I get fish and chips?*

On the subject of fish and chips, it seems that you have to have fish and chips. If you order a fish and a bag of chips you will always get the two together even if you want them and ask for them separately. Some people will have say fish and mushy peas whilst their friend wants sausage and chips. Almost always the fish and the chips will be wrapped together. It's as if the two words are inseparable. I suppose this is just force of habit but I like to think of it as dialect by deed.

What's your name? A common enough question. Or maybe *What's his name?* referring to a baby in a pram. I have a job with this one – I just want to say *John.* French people learning English are taught *My name is John* but we have to learn the French *je m'appelle John.* Where is this getting us? I hear you ask. Well what does a Hull person say in reply to your question? *They call me John* or *They call him John.* Even when your baby is newborn and you've only just given him or her a name it's still *They call him John* even though it's you who've called him it. And the question to ask the new mother is *What do they call him?* Je m'appelle translates as I call myself; slightly different but I would have thought the same derivation, so has Hull quietly nicked something from the French? That I doubt but you'll rarely hear *My name is John* on the streets of the city.

What about adverts? We usually call them adverts don't we? But what do we call the long word? Advertisements. Yes that's right but how do we pronounce it? In Hull it is adver**tize**ments but in the rest of the known universe it is ad**ver**tissments.

Similarly who do we get in a factory or an office to replace a faulty lightbulb? We get Maintenance don't we? Except in our fair city where we call *Main**tain**ance.*

Then there is the Summer Fair or Fayre (not the Christmas Fayre described earlier!) or, in some places, the carnival. Think of another name for it - to many it is a *gala*, you know – it rhymes with parlour. Nevertheless many Hull people say it as if it rhymes with sailor.

I have to find a place for the word *mauve* – you know that kind of pale purple colour. It's not universal but quite a lot of Hull people pronounce it as if it were spelt *morv*. The rest, albeit with the accent that gives us *home* and *Frome Road*, pronounce it *moav* (to rhyme with cove) in line with the rest of the country.

I travelled a lot by bus in the first few years that I lived in East Yorkshire – mainly the 3 and the 4 as they were then to and from Hull city centre. Often, in rush hours, East Yorkshire and Hull Corporation would put on an extra bus to cope with demand. This would run behind or in front of the main bus until they reached a point where the number of passengers had reduced and they would all fit on the one bus. Now where I lived as a child, and also in London where there always seems to be more buses than anywhere in the world, this extra bus was called the *relief*. Not in Hull! of course not, we had our own word for it. It was the *Duplicate*.

The other cutie that has come to my attention goes back to pronunciation. Not everyone uses this but with some people it is really prominent. I am describing the way some Hull people pronounce the word *sure*. It seems to have evolved in most of the country to sound similar if not identical to the word *shore* but in some Hull people's conversation it has two very distinct syllables and comes out, with a definite stress on the first syllable, as *shoo-wer*

CHAPTER   THIRTEEN

Words

I leave until last the selection of words that are unique to or at least typical of the Hull dialect. As I have hinted before, this is the part that first caught my interest as a teenager and has remained a fascination ever since. Unfortunately it is very hard to work out which words are actually unique to Hull as some that have been quoted to me are in use in other places. I have looked at words used in Doncaster though, which is less than fifty miles from Hull and it is remarkable how many words are different. At the same time some of the words that I thought and have been assured by others to be pure Hull are actually used there too, or even further away in some cases. I have therefore included some that fall into those categories, with an accompanying comment.

I guess these words and for that matter all the words used in the various dialects that make the English language so rich have evolved over many years in the same way as Darwin described evolution in the world of nature; by that I mean natural selection. In the case of words, when there might have been several for the same thing, perhaps each coming in from a different country or culture, it would be the one used the most often or by the most people that would survive. Therefore I assume that more people in Hull said bread cake and more in London called it a roll and that is why those names remain today.

It is difficult to think of a sensible order to list these so in general they are in alphabetical order except where similarity makes putting two together more logical. As you can see, there is no theme, no logic in these words. Very few have any relationship with another so you get a whole range of vocabulary referring to a given subject amongst which we find one word that is unique, different or just plain peculiar. Here goes then:

Agonising. It's agonising = It hurts badly. This is a contradiction of the normal Hull thing of shortening words in that it lengthens the word agony. Not only that but it converts the adjective into a verb too. It's a good start.

Back kitchen. The kitchen in most Hull houses is more often than not referred to as the back kitchen. It seems strange as there is not a front kitchen so there is no need to differentiate. There was often a front room (which in many cases was rarely used, despite many of the houses being extremely small and cramped) so maybe it was the opposite of that. Quite a few houses that were built towards the end of the twentieth century actually have the kitchen next to the front door. Unfortunately I don't know anyone who lives in one of these to ask if they still call it the back kitchen. Maybe I should go and knock on people's doors asking what they call their kitchen. Perhaps not.

Backstump. This is a term used for the wicketkeeper in a game of cricket. I had heard backstop, meaning someone standing behind the keeper to try and stop what he misses but where backstump comes from I know not. Incidentally the expression I used to hear "down south" is Wicky.

Bains also **Granbains**. This is a derivation of bairns which is usually associated with Scotland but is used as near to Hull as Doncaster, albeit with a different pronunciation of course. It refers of course to children. *I'm taking the bain to school.* This is one of the wonderfully-pronounced words if you have a Hull accent and is virtually impossible to mimic if you haven't. It is also quite common to refer to your child as *the bain* in the same way as people say *the wife.* I don't like that. Makes it seem like a possession, a thing rather than a much loved fellow human.

Baking Apples. Yes these are what everyone else calls cooking apples. Bramleys are the undisputed best but there are others.

Bauk. - maybe it would be spelt **bork** or **balk** meaning to be sick / nauseous / reach / retch. *The smell of curry makes me bauk.* Or more to the point listening to Bjork makes me – er - bjork

Beer Off. Yes the Beer Off is the off license, a kind of shop that is fast disappearing under the ever-looming hand of the giant supermarkets. Formerly staffed exclusively by people who were incapable of assessing anyone's age, they are now becoming increasingly rare as attempts are made to reduce teenage drinking. The police now use underage people to attempt to buy alcoholic drinks then smack the proverbial botties of those who sell to them without asking for ID. There must be a better way to do this.

Boule or possibly **bool** – to push along – a bike, a shopping trolley or a pram for example. Basically anything on wheels that is pushed, even a hula hoop on its way to wherever hula hoops are – er – hula hooped. *Just bool that along to Auntie Ethel's will you.*

Bonny – good looking as in a baby or pretty, attractive, as in a girl. This is very Scottish and the often-heard *she's a bonny lass* is even more so, though this is stereotypically a Geordie expression. Bonny is heard in South Yorkshire as well so is plainly not just a Hull word but it is in very common use. In Sheffield, however, it can mean chubby when referred to a baby or healthy-looking which apparently a chubby baby is. Would a teenage girl who was described as chubby be also thought of healthy-looking? Somehow I think not so maybe we've got this one right in Hull.

Bramble. A bramble is a prickly bush which has rather tasty black berries which, with a huge dollop of originality, are called blackberries. Except in Hull where the berries are called brambles. The thought of a bramble pie is horrible – you'd tear the inside of tour mouth to shreds. So what do Hull people call the bramble if they call the blackberries brambles? A bramble bush I assume.

Bray. Meaning to beat, hit or smack. *If you go to the Millwall match you'll get a good braying* or, to a child perhaps, *Cut that out or I'll bray you.* I think I've scoured more dictionaries and websites for an explanation of this word than any other but to no avail. It does have at least four meanings that are referred to fairly consistently: (1) The sound made by a donkey, (2) To laugh loudly and harshly (I suppose Guffaw rather than eeyore), (3) To pound or crush fine, as in a mortar and (4) To spread ink thinly onto a plate before placing onto a printing press.

So a fine, useful word with many meanings, none of which bear any resemblance to the Hull meaning. It's comforting to know that, if someone is told that they are coming to Hull for a braying, they won't be subjected to a load of donkey noises or a demonstration of the invention of Herr Gütenberg; merely a sound beating.

Bread Cakes. One of the great fascinations of English is bread as it has all sorts of names all over the country. There are rolls, baps, buns, stotties, teacakes, barm cakes and more. In Hull if you ask for a sandwich you will almost certainly expect and get your choice of filling in a *bread cake*. If you want sliced bread or something similar you would ask for a sandwich on (not in) sliced bread. If the shop has run out of *cakes* the staff will probably apologise and ask if it's OK on sliced bread. If you ask for a sandwich in London you will get sliced bread. If you want a roll (a bread cake to Hull people) you ask for a cheese roll – assuming of course that you want cheese but you get the drift. Are you still with me? Good, as this leads us on nicely to the expressions *bacon cakes* and *sausage cakes* which are used, certainly in East Hull and are an anathema to people from almost anywhere else to whom a cake is definitely sweet not savoury. Just to add to the confusion, in some parts of the country, a bun is a bread roll / bread cake but in other places a bun is a sweet pastry or small cake. Talk about complicated. A nice aside to this is the lovely Hull request for no butter in your sandwich – *Have you got a cheese sandwich on a dry cake?*

Chow at you. Loosely speaking this is a telling off. *If I stop at the pub on the way home I'll get chowed at. Don't do that in class or Mr Smith will chow at you.* Try as I may I can find nothing to explain the origins of this word and no sign of its use anywhere else. Let's just take it as a word that is pure Hull.

Cockle over. Lots of people have told me that this is a Hull expression but it takes very little in the way of investigation to discover that it is not. It is in fact used all over the country and there is even a legal case of a workman who got compensation from one of those (adjective deleted) No Win No Fee solicitors because he *cockled over* whilst laying some roof tiles. So, sorry – not this one.

Coggy. Not a very common one this but I've heard it used for the crust at the end of a loaf of bread, especially a crusty one or a French stick. The bit that breaks bits off your fillings when you bite on it or gets stuck vertically between your teeth.

Corporation House. Hull has what is claimed to be the biggest Council Estate in Europe, or even the world, in Bransholme, as well as a number of other fairly large council estates. People in Hull, nevertheless, do not live in council houses, they live in *corporation houses*. This goes back to the days when buses had *Corporation Transport* on the side and the city council was known to many as Hull Corporation. Yes, council house is the word in the rest of England but it's Corporation House in Hull.

Croggy. A croggy is a ride on the cross-bar of a bike though it has come to mean a ride on any part of the bike, often on the saddle whilst the poor person pedalling has to stand. Those of us who took notice when we did our cycling proficiency test will know that it is illegal but it is an every day, no a several times a day occurrence. I've never quite worked out how you do it so I can't write from experience here but it does seem to me to be a fairly big sacrifice on the part of the owner / rider of the bike who has to pedal twice as hard whilst his passenger does very little, except hang on for dear life.

Cutfish. I mentioned cutfish at the beginning of the book. I'm not aware of any fish and chip shop that still offers this indeterminate delicacy. I haven't been to anywhere near all of the chip shops in the city, nor for the sake of my somewhat delicate digestive system do I have any intention of doing so;--

Some of them it's bad enough walking past and smelling the stuff they cook the fish and chips in never mind actually going in and spending money. It has never ceased to amaze me, though, that the people in what was the country's major fishing port seemed unaware of what they were actually eating. In fact this is still the case in quite a few of these august establishments. Even though we no longer have our old friend cutfish, there are still shops where it just says *Fish* on the price list so the opportunity both to choose our preferred fish and actually know what it is we are eating is denied us. Perhaps I have answered my own question and the cooking fat destroyed any semblance of flavour or at the very least ensured that everything tasted more or less the same. But, as I said at the beginning of the book, when I asked what cutfish was in a fish and chip shop soon after I moved from "down south", *It's fish – that's been cut.*

Diddlum. What a lovely word. Have you ever been asked *Are you in the diddlum this year?* It's what everyone else knows as a Christmas Club where a group of people, colleagues or neighbours for example, all put in a bit of money each week or each month which gets put in a savings account in a bank and the person who organises it takes the money all out and shares it round, with interest, a few weeks before Christmas.

Drain. When I first heard that children were playing or fishing in the drain I was horrified. I probably needn't have bothered as the word drain, in Hull, refers to a series of canals that were built around the late 18th and early 19th centuries to improve the drainage of farmland in East Yorkshire. Many of these flow into the River Hull or the Humber on their way to the sea. One can only wonder what the effect might have been in June 2007 had they all still existed and been in a good state of repair. The city might not have suffered the devastating floods.

One of the more well-known drains is the Beverley and Barmston Drain, known locally as Barmston Drain or, to use Hull's penchant for shortening names, Barmy Drain. In the past it was also often known as Lecky Drain because, as it flowed through the city, it passed beside a power station. No -

hold on a minute – what I mean is a power station was built beside it. In any case the effect of the power station was to warm the water and make it into a kind of heated swimming pool. No Health and Safety people again in those days. It was used for both swimming and fishing at least up to the 1960s.

Eggitybudge. Known in other places by names such as Eggy Moo or Bad Eggs, Eggitybudge is the Hull version of a children's game. There seems to be an almost infinite number of versions of it but basically it involves one child throwing a ball in the air and another one catching or otherwise retrieving it whilst various things are shouted. This may be in the form of a quiz such as name as many things in a category before the ball gets back or similar. In one version the ball was thrown against a wall, or in the air and if the person selected could catch the ball before it hit the ground they cried 'Fry your own bacon' and the 'it' was still 'it'. In another version, one player threw a ball in the air and called another one's name. Everyone else ran away. When the kid who was named retrieved the ball they called out 'eggity budge' and everyone else froze. He could then throw the ball at or for another child. The target child could dodge the ball as it was "Bad egg if you budge' - eggity budge. As I said, almost as many versions as there were children. I wonder if it is played nowadays?. Maybe there's a virtual version.

Faff. I think I have been told I should include Faff in this book by more people than any other word but it isn't a Hull word. It's in common use all over the country. We all faff or faff about, wherever we come from. And let's face it we do don't we?

Fast. Here's an interesting one that I didn't come across for a few years after my immigration to East Yorkshire though I have heard it a lot since. Remembering (for those who don't have a Hull accent) that it rhymes with gassed, fast in this case means stuck. I suppose it's a derivation of fastened but it's in common use – *I can't turn round, my zip's fast* or maybe *he's got his foot fast in the railings.* Taking it to its logical conclusion this means that it must be possible to be slow because something is fast.

Foggy. I'd love to find the derivation of this delightful word meaning first. Maybe it's simply a shortening (in the same logical way that the name Debra is shortened to Debbie) of the Hull pronunciation of *first* which sometimes comes out as *fost*. I haven't heard it myself but my research tells me that there are also instances of *seggy* being used to mean second. I have heard children shout *bags foggy* meaning *please may I go first* in a game but not *bags seggy* or bags anything else.... except *bags laggy* meaning please may I go last.

Gen. Pronounced with a hard *g*, I take this to be a corruption of the word *against*. It is used to mean *beside* or *next door to*. A woman interviewed on local television said that she went to the hairdressers *gen* the chip shop.

Goodies. No, not an iconic 1970s comedy but goodies are what the people of Hull call sweets and the Americans call candy. We have a goodie jar in our house that is filled with bars of chocolate or packs of fruit gums or smarties. Just about anything you can buy from a sweet shop would come under the heading of goodies. I have recently been contacted by a lady who said that, when children were very young, they would be referred to as googoos.

Handles on a clock. I'm not sure if this is dialect or pure ignorance. I've heard it said a few times and always in the Hull area so I've got to go for dialect. I really hate this one because, even if it is dialect, it makes the speaker seem thick and the whole fascination with dialects is that some of the cleverest, most educated people have them.

Bringing to mind the use of this turn of phrase reminds me of the occasion when I was treated to the use of another completely wrong expression that I **can** only put down to the speaker being thick. Asking if I could play the piano in a well known Hull hotel not a million miles from the railway station, I was told by the receptionist that I couldn't because *it's not tuned in*. I felt like saying I wanted to play the piano not listen to the radio but I just walked out shaking my head.

Hard on. Yes this is the Hull expression for sound asleep. *He was hard on when she came to bed.*

Laggy band. Here we have another one that I would love to be Hull only but I'm afraid it isn't, despite a number of people insisting that it is. Once again, sorry, it's in regular usage in Hull but it is also found dotted about the whole country. Two uses therefore of the word *laggy*. See *Foggy* above.

Kegs. Nothing to do with barrels, even of the (un)lamented Hull Brewery. Your kegs are your trousers or occasionally whatever you choose to wear underneath your trousers. Apparently in other parts of the north the word *keks* is used. *I bought a pair of kegs from marksiz.*

Lark. The verb to lark is, in Hull, the same as to play. So we hear *Are you larkin?* or *Wagstaff was a good larker.* It's perfectly acceptable around the country and can be found in various dictionaries, to say *lark about*, meaning to frolick or to play pranks, something that might be described as a bit of a lark, but the Hull usage suggests something a bit more formal than that, even more so with the description of well-known sportsmen. In some parts of the country the word laking is used but larking seems sufficiently Hull to count here.

Legging-up day. After 12 noon on April 1st it ceases to be April Fools' Day and becomes Legging-up Day. Apparently this means you can go round tripping people up more or less willy nilly. I have to say I find this one of the more unsavoury aspects of life in Hull if only for the fact that, if it happened to me I would be bound to land in a puddle. In most of the rest of the country it is something simple like if you do a prank after mid-day it's you who is the fool. Wow that's exciting. But in Hull it is open day for what can only be described as assault.

Lugs. Are what you or your cat get in your hair when it is all knotted up. If your hair is taffled up (see below), it may be in lugs. Probably it needs to be washed and brushed (*needs washing and brushing* – remember those present participles!) Anywhere else in the country your lugs are your ears as in your lugholes.

Mafted. There's a lovely word – *Will you open the window, I'm mafted.* It means very hot, perhaps sweating, certainly uncomfortable. It is actually a word that is not unique to Hull and seems to be found in a number of pockets right up the North East coast. There is a similar word in use in South Yorkshire – maffin' meaning hot and clammy weather but this makes for further confusion as, OK, I'd always thought of the word clammy to mean hot and sticky – i.e. the type of weather that might make you feel *mafted* but Websters Dictionary describes clammy as feeling cold and damp.

Mash the tea. Now I'm not a tea drinker and I have had a lot of stick over the years from people who don't like the way that I make tea. Milk in first, milk in last, too much milk, not enough milk, too strong, too weak; you can't win with tea If you make it how you like it, your guests will object, if you make it how one guest likes it your second guest will object. One thing is certain though, when you've put the tea and the boiling water into the teapot you leave it for a while before you pour it out into cups or mugs to drink. The argument here is what you leave it to do. You leave it to stand in the pot don't you? OK but I was brought up to leave it to draw and I have occasionally been asked to leave it to brew. Not in Hull though. In Hull, and unfortunately in a few other places, parts of Derbyshire for sure, you leave it to mash. I say unfortunately as it would be lovely if this was unique to Hull. I don't get this one at all, mash has a definite meaning and it's to do with potatoes or swedes. Alright it has a second meaning if you're a fan of American sitcoms but tea? I suppose it's out of the question to say *I'll just leave the tea to infuse* or something like that. There is further confusion in that, to some people, if you leave it in for too long it will stew but that's another story.

Mend the fire. Here's another expression that people seem to think is unique to Hull but isn't. It's still well used and worth mentioning though. To mend the fire means to put on more coal or logs. I think it only refers to a fire in your house, I've never heard of mending the fire of a railway engine. It seems a strange expression again as the word *mend* has a definite meaning and, to me, to mend the fire would require it to be broken in the first place.

To go off at a tangent for a moment, the expression *mend the fire* can be found in the poem *The Clock is on the Stroke of Six* by Mary Howitt who had several claims to fame – she wrote *Will you come into my parlour said the spider to the fly* and *Hush little baby don't you cry* as well as translating a lot of the works of Hans Christian Andersen. Yet again a book about the Hull dialect is educational? I won't let the fruits of my research go to waste. It's just a shame that she came from Gloucestershire.

Mister. Most of the things I have discovered in my journey through the Hull dialect fall into the category of fascination, that is to say I am really interested and gain pleasure from listening to them or working them out. The odd one, however, really annoys me and, just like *I aren't*, one that truly grates is the use of the word *mister* as a noun. *Go and ask that mister for an ice cream.* What?! We have mothers telling young children to call a man (1 syllable, 3 letters) a mister (2 syllables, 6 letters). No wonder we have poor results in English language. Why can't we use the word *man*? It's a perfectly good word and they wouldn't say it to an adult would they? Which leads us nicely onto a conundrum; at what age do parents stop calling a man a mister? Do the children come home from school one day and say, *Mummy I've learned a new word today – man – it's what you tell me to call a mister?* It's a bit like the old one whereby you can tell if someone is old or not because, if they are old, they have a fall. Younger people fall over. But at what point does it change?

To neb or be nebby. If you stand close to somebody who is on the phone, they might turn to you and say *Stop nebbing*, because it's Hull speak for being nosey, listening in or eavesdropping. Not only that but this word has a proper derivation as both Scottish and middle English can be traced back to the word *neb* meaning either a bird's beak or an animal's (and logically therefore a person's) nose. Hence nebby = nosey. Well, we've reached N in the alphabet and found something logical.

Nunty. Nunty means old fashioned in the sense of someone or something's appearance. *That dress is a bit nunty*, or *She's got a bit of a nunty hairstyle*. It seems to refer to someone whose appearance makes them look drab, or older than they are; in a way lamb dressed up as mutton. Does it only apply to women or women's clothes I wonder. You don't hear *that Ford Cortina is a bit nunty*.

Our lass. This is one of the Hull greats. Everybody knows the regular Northern use of *Our Johnny. Our Sue* etc, if only from watching Cilla Black on the TV (*Our Jack was breech you know*). But Our Lass is the Hull way of saying my wife or my girlfriend. There is no male equivalent. Thank goodness. I don't like it but it soars way above the frequently-used alternative *the wife*. As I said before, if you have any inkling of respect for your good lady it should be <u>my</u> wife not <u>the</u> wife. Sermon over.

Our kid. Strangely enough, living alongside *our lass* is another Hullism but which this time is male and has no female equivalent. *Our kid* is my brother; usually, but not always, my younger brother. *If you've got a spare ticket our kid'll have it*. Even when both brothers are adult, *Our kid* still applies. I know a man who is in his 50s who goes to football every week with *Our kid*.

Pack ups. When they do the register at school, the children have to shout out either lunch or pack ups. I have found several definitions of pack up in at least three different dictionaries but not one of them makes the slightest reference to the Hull meaning. Pack up means sandwiches or, to get nearer to the words themselves, a packed lunch. *We'll pack up* or *We'll take a pack up* seem to be used with about the same frequency. There's a kind of logic in that it can mean any kind of food that you might take to eat around what in Hull and several other areas is dinner time but in other places is lunch time. If you say *sandwiches* then, if you take a bag of crisps and a sausage roll, you are not describing it correctly. That's where good old *pack up* comes in; it is all-encompassing. Not only that but you can have a pack up for tea, for breakfast or any other time that suits you. At least one primary school has a *pack up trolley* where they are all kept. What a fine expression.

Patties. Yes patties are from Hull. *Patty and chips twice please.* There is some argument about how they are made – I was told some time ago that yesterday's left over fish and potato probably sums it up best but I have been told several times since that there is certainly no fish involved - but whatever and however you won't find a patty in a chip shop more than a few miles from Hull. You can get them in Beverley, though I have been assured that you can't, but you can't get them in York. There is a thing called a patty or a fish patty which is available in other parts of the country but is something entirely different from the "Hull Patty". A particular delicacy of the Hull populace, ever keen on healthy eating, is the Patty Butty or even a patty butty and chips.

Pennies. It's high horse dismounting time again. Here's another real bugbear. For some reason it is common to describe money to young children as pennies. How are the poor schoolteachers supposed to explain money when the children are brought up to call everything pennies? It's a good job we don't still have half-crowns, florins, shillings, groats, farthings etc or we'd never be able to buy anything for the right price. What we do have now is just about the worst sentence that any Hull parent can utter. Yes it must be *Give your pennies to the mister.* In the words of Freddie Mercury, *No, no, no, no, no, no no! Give your money to the man.*

Pikelets. It's taken more effort to work this one out than all the others put together and I still haven't got a definitive answer. Basically a pikelet is what Hull people call what some other people call a crumpet or possibly a muffin. But it's not as simple as that because there are wide differences between what people around the country (and for that matter around the world) call both a muffin and a crumpet. Clear? No it isn't. Go to any of the well-known supermarkets whose mispronounced names we talked about earlier in the book and buy a packet of pikelets – what does it say on the pack? Crumpets. Nowhere will it say pikelets. I have found that in some places a pikelet is similar to a pancake, the main difference with a pikelet is that self-raising flour is used instead of plain. However a look in the dictionary defines a pikelet as a small thick pancake found in Australia and New Zealand.

Confused? Well think of the old children's song *I am the muffin man,* this is hundreds of years old yet nowadays if you go to the shops for a muffin you'll get the American type of cupcake that are in all the bakers and coffee shops nowadays.

However perhaps the ultimate clearing up of this confusion comes from a website that I found that I think was trying to translate English to Japanese and vice versa and help Japanese people understand English. Or not.

> The crumpet is circular in shape (usually; long and square varieties also exist) and has a distinctive flat top covered in small holes. It has a resilient, slightly spongy texture and a rather bland flavour which, when eaten hot with a topping (usually butter), together make crumpets crisp on the outside and very succulent on the inside. Crumpets are still one of the mainstays of the English breakfast table. They differ from the English Muffin, which is cooked on both sides, in that the dough is usually more moist to start with, so that a muffin ring may be required to hold the batter's shape
>
> Crumpets are served hot, usually with butter. Other popular accompaniments include jam, Marmite, honey, or cheese. Typically, several crumpets are brought together and toasted. A pikelet is similar to a crumpet, but much thinner and sometimes irregularly shaped. However, the meaning of pikelet varies: in some regions of Britain it traditionally refers to a crumpet, muffin or other teacake. In Australia and New Zealand it refers to a Scotch pancake.

So there you go, none of these describe what Hull people call a pikelet but at least it gives us a few alternatives. Or does it? Just go and buy a pack of crumpets but make sure you call them something else.

Pot. No not something you shouldn't smoke despite what Paul McCartney might tell you. And no not *the pots* (see *wash the pots* below). A pot is the thing they put on your arm or your leg in hospital when you've broken said limb. I was brought up to call it a *plaster*, in Lancashire it's a *plastercast* and in London it's a *cast*. A select group of people in North London had no idea that it was a pot until they met someone from Hull. It's sometimes referred to as a pot leg or a pot arm but it would seem that pot is a Hull word.

Reallio. This is a playground game where you basically had two teams, one team were the chasers and they had to try to catch all the other team and take them to a base where they had to stay until all of their team had been caught. However they could link hands and form a long chain reaching outside of the base and if a remaining "free" team member was able run or sneak up and touch this chain then the whole team was free again. Sort of the thinking man's kiss chase.

Rully man or **Rulley man.** We mentioned this is the chapter about fishing but it probably needs to be here too as it was wider-ranging than the fish dock. This was in effect a man with a horse and cart. There were several places where rulleymen could be found but examples as well as the fish dock were the fruit market and railway stations and goods yards. He might deliver to customers on behalf of a business or he might be just employed to move things around, say from the auction to the trains or lorries that will take them to their destinations.

Runners in. Frequently written as *runner's in* are often wanted by Hull taxi and private hire companies. I spent months, no, years trying to discover the meaning of this expression; I asked a number of people who work in taxi offices and they didn't know and, when I was younger and more naive I used to think it was when a taxi firm has just bought a brand new car and they were looking after the engine. So I am grateful to a young lady from a local taxi firm who Emailed me this; *My understanding of the meaning is when a taxi driver works from an office as he is self-employed and keeps the money received from the customers but he pays a weekly amount of "running in" for the work he receives from the office.* Thanks Rachel. I think I understand.

Sannies. Yes, this is the one that set it off all those years ago. *Me sannies are brannies*, someone said and I really wish I could remember who it was so I could give them their due credit for both this book and a lifetime of enjoyment. The shoes that Hull people use for PE at school are among those things that have many names across the country - usually gym shoes or plimsolls. In fact the word *sannies* is really an abbreviation of sand shoes, a name which is in use equally as frequently. How many Hull schools have sand in their hall or gym is debatable but if you find one that does, you can be sure that the children will be well prepared.

Set the table. Prepare the table for a meal or, as I was brought up to say, lay the table. Here we have an expression where, in stark contrast to some of those above, like mend the fire, is actually more logical in the Hull usage than the so-called correct version. I suppose you do carefully lay knives and forks on a table but *set the table* somehow evokes putting everything in the right place. Go Hull!

Siling Down. If it is siling down it is raining heavily. It, of course, meaning the weather - we all say *what's it like?* when we mean what is the weather like. There are plenty of other expressions that are in common usage for this meteorological experience, some less polite then others but, for Hull people, or at least polite Hull people, siling down will do. Well after I did most of my research into the Hull dialect, someone suggested that this expression originates from rain beating against grain silos or similar in East Hull or Holderness.

Skeg. As with a few of these words, I wish skeg was a truly Hull word but it crops up in several places although the wonderful font of all knowledge that is Wikipedia describes it as a Hull word. Worldwide it is the word for the bit that sticks out of the back of a boat to accommodate a rudder. Even more confusingly it apparently means beard, so Skegness in old Norse meant beard point. In Hull however it is always as a noun meaning a look as in *let's have a skeg at that*. This usage does appear to originate from Hull so we can claim it as a Hull word. All the references I have looked up describe it as

Hull and Yorkshire usage or words to that effect so it's good enough for me.

Spanish and Kaylie pronounced Kay-Lie but sometimes spelt khali, so it ought to rhyme with khaki but doesn't, are two examples of goodies as mentioned above. Spanish is what the rest of the English-speaking world call liquorice – though an awful lot of them pronounce it *lickerish* – those horrible smelling and worse tasting black stringy things that you can buy in sweet shops. I'd really love these two words to be native to Hull but, unfortunately they're not. I have found usage of Spanish in the North East, in Lancashire and, fairly predictably in West Yorkshire, in particular Pontefract where Pontefract Cakes were made of the stuff – maybe they still are.

There is a story behind this which seems to vary from place to place. It may be because the stuff was imported from Spain or it may be because some monks brought a liquorice tree from Spain to Riveaulx Abbey and it spread around the North from there. It was actually grown around Pontefract as well so choose your own derivation. Kaylie on the other hand is powdered sherbet. Or maybe it isn't, maybe it's flavoured sugar. Everywhere you look and everyone you ask you get a different description. Whatever, it seems that you dipped your Spanish into your Kaylie and then popped it into your mouth inducing what the advertising blurb referred to as a pleasant sensation. It just goes to show how hard life was in the North if that was considered pleasant.

Spell. This is nothing to do with getting the letters in words in the correct order – something which the population of Hull are statistically very poor at – though that's an entirely different subject which I will steer away from as I actually want the good people of the city on my side. Neither is it something that you go or are put under by a witch, a wizard or perhaps a particularly good singer. Here in our wonderful city, a spell is a noun meaning a splinter as in one of those annoying small pieces of wood that get into your skin when you are mending your fence. Assuming you've got a fence of course. My limited research suggests the use of the work *spelk* in the north east and parts of Scotland but spell seems to be Hull-orientated.

Sprag is the Hull verb meaning to tell tales or to report someone or something to authority. It is in regular use in Hull but is also found in parts of Lincolnshire and, bizarrely, in Macclesfield. *If you do that I'll sprag on you.* It is a word with more than one meaning in the dictionary; always however a noun rather than a verb. It can be something used to prevent a vehicle from moving - a choc if you like – possibly a piece of wood or metal wedged beneath a wheel or between spokes or a pointed stake lowered at an angle into the ground. In a similar vein a sprag in some parts of the country is a pit prop – also a pointed stick stuck into the ground.

An interesting Hull connection is that, in some places, a young cod is referred to as a sprag. Not a codling which is a very young fish but one not fully grown or developed, perhaps 5 years old. A cod might be a fish longer than 30" 6cm) whereas a sprag would be between 25" and 30" (63 – 75cm) and a codling smaller than that. The similar word for a salmon or a trout is a smolt.

Taffled Have you ever put a load of electrical cables away, carefully winding them individually then gone back to them in a day or so and they appear to be wound up in each other? Of course you have and do you know what? – if you're from Hull you'll say that they are *taffled* or maybe *taffled up* - we like pointless prepositions. All sorts of things can get taffled - hair or wool or wire or string and the dictionary word would be tangled though most people would say tangled up. I'm pretty sure this is a Hull one as it's not on any of the lists of slang words that I have found. Using some kind of logic there should be, and of course there is, an opposite which, no surprise here, is the verb to untaffle. So you might hear *I need to untaffle my laces.*

Tansad. One of the best things about writing this is the odd little surprises that keep popping up. Tansad is one of them. I've lost count of the number of people who have said to me that they either took their children or were taken as children in a tansad when what they mean is a pram or pushchair or buggy, whichever term you prefer to use nowadays. Now settle down to be disappointed all you older Hull people but tansad is not a Hull word. There was a company which was trading, certainly from the First World War onwards in Birmingham called Tansad Ltd who manufactured, among other things, *baby carriages and folding perambulators.*

Grace's Guide shows Tansad as exhibitors in the British Industries fairs of 1922 and 1929. In 1922 they were manufacturers of Tan-Sad Typists' Tables; Constructional Toys; Motor Cycle Pillion Seats and Saddles, and Super Sprung Perambulators; Tan-Sad Chairs for Workers (Office or Factory). By 1929 they were a bit more outgoing and described themselves as manufacturers of Wheel Toys in wood and metal. Baby Carriages and Folding Perambulators; Folding Invalid Chairs; Pillion Seats and Accessories for Motor Cycles. Steel Chairs for office and factory workers, and steel and Wood Folding Chairs for the home.

Not only that but the word is equally at home in France. A French / English dictionary comes up with: **Tansad.** *(Mot anglais) Nom masculin singulier. Siège du passager d'un cheval ou d'une motocyclette* or if you prefer *(English word) pillion, extra seat behind the saddle of a horse or motorcycle.*

So now we are left with a conundrum. Is Tansad another of those words that takes its name from a manufacturer and is then used to describe everything similar even if made by someone else? Like Hoover. We all do the hoovering even if we use a Henry or a Dyson or Curry's own make. To be honest I don't know but the research has been fascinating and I will share a bit more with you.

Tansad had some lovely slogans on their advertisements, some of which would be frowned upon today. *Carry Her in Comfort* from 1919 referred to the pillion seat on a motorbike. No thought in those days that she might be the rider carrying him! By 1932 you could *Fit a Tansad* offering comfort and safety for 30 shillings.

Tansad Ltd were still trading in the 1950s though in 1931 they were taken over by Avery, the Scales people and renamed the Tansad Chair Company (1931) Ltd. More recently at an auction one of the lots was described as a "Tansad" 1950s Rexine covered metal framed folding pushchair.

So Somewhere along the line the word Tansad, in Hull, came to mean a particular type of pram, possibly one that could be folded and was more portable than the large wheeled Silver Cross types. So not a Hull word but one that came to have a specific meaning in Hull. Don't say this book isn't informative.

Tenfoot. According to Simon Elmes's book "Talking for Britain" the humble passageway between two rows of houses or from one adjacent area to another has more synonyms than almost anything else in the English language. Some are found in several parts of the country but Tenfoot is unique to Hull. Some of the other words are ginnell (pronounced with either a hard or a soft g), alley, snicket, lane, twitten, jitty, even entry. Tenfoot, unlike tansad, we can claim for Hull. Allegedly they are actually ten feet wide. Apparently there are eight-foots in Grimsby. Then again Grimsby always was a small version of Hull.

Tipple Tail. This refers to the gymnastic or, if you prefer, contortionist act otherwise known as Head over Heels at least this was what I was taught to call it when I was a child – or, more to the point, where I was as a child. Tipple tail makes a lot more sense because the act actually requires your heels to go over your head, head over heels describing their normal relative position. In the Cubs it was called a somersault, but I was reliably informed that the correct gymnastic term is a Forward Roll. Whatever, it involves the body going through 360 degrees. I quite like tipple tail, it certainly makes more sense than head over heels. Stupid southerners – oh I'm one of them aren't I?

Treacle is a word used in Hull to mean Golden Syrup. This is kind of logical as we use Golden Syrup to make treacle Pudding but is Golden Syrup the same as treacle? I can probably do no better than quote the website of Lyle's who manufacture the stuff. It says no, they're very different in taste, texture and appearance, but in some parts of the UK, especially in the north of England, some people call golden syrup 'treacle'. Treacle tarts are, in fact, made with golden syrup. How much of the north of England though? Certainly Hull.

Tret and Pled. Tret is the past participle of the verb to treat. We always thought it was treated but in Hull it's tret. *I thought we were tret very badly.* I can understand how this may have come about as it's easier on the ear and the tongue than treated. It can also be *My boyfriend tret me to a meal out.*

On a similar tack, on a BBC Radio Humberside program in April 2009 that well-known eloquent sports presenter and Rugby League expert Gwillym Lloyd stated that a certain person had *pled guilty* in court. That was the first and only time I have heard pled as the past participle of the verb to plead. There is a certain logic if you think of the past participles of the verbs to bleed, to feed or to speed. I'm not so sure about going to weed the garden though. Despite his name Gwillym is pure Hull. Well if he wasn't he is now after speaking like that.

Tut shops. I'm not so sure about this one as I've only heard two people use it, my wife and my mother-in-law. Having said that, when I've asked what it meant some Hull people seemed to know. They are the bucket and spade / souvenir shops on the sea front at resorts like Scarborough or Bridlington, though the name still applies in Torquay or Tenerife.

Twag. To twag is to play truant. Alternatively *He's twaggin'it.* This is another word which has all sorts of synonyms around the country. *Bunking off* is quite common, *playing hooky, bobbing, wagging, skiving, skidging,* or *beaking* are all in use around the country and I'm sure there are many others. Unfortunately Hull has a very high incidence of truancy so the word twag is in pretty common usage.

Wash the pots. Alternatively **Do the pots**. This is the Hull term for what I always knew as *do the washing up,* washing up being entirely distinct from washing. Yes after every meal there is, or was in the days before electric dishwashers and student flats, a requirement to clean all the crockery, cutlery and cooking utensils that have been used during the preparing, cooking, serving and eating of the meal. As we know this is generally referred to as doing the washing up but in Hull we *do the pots*. Why is this? At some time all those things made out of bone china, finest Sheffield steel, wood, plastic, glass etc. suddenly metamorphose into *pots.* Then once they have been washed, or *done,* they stop being pots and get put away in their relevant home. Even when you go into a shop to buy them they are not pots, it's just for that short period of time whilst they are being washed or waiting to be washed – then – and only then – they are pots.

Yon end / yon side. The other end or the far side. *Just boule this down yon end.* Isn't that a lovely expression? Just take it down to the other end is accurate but it lacks the charm of the colloquialism. *Marksiz is on yon side of the road.* Brilliant.

CHAPTER FOURTEEN

Conclusion

So ends our little list of words and phrases that stand out as Hullisms. Well no because that's a word I made up but they bind together to make that wonderful thing that is the Hull dialect. For some reason Hull, in its place at the end of the railway line, the end of the motorway, where you only go to, never through, has developed its own way of speaking. Its own way of embellishing this wonderful language we bandy together and call English. It's just that nobody seems to know.

I've talked to countless people, read books and articles, listened to local radio and scanned the internet and I think I am accurate in my statements above. Please, dear reader, if you have reached this far, let me know if I am right or wrong and, if you know of any other words that I have missed out please tell me. There are several that I have been told, or thought myself to be Hull only that I have investigated and found to be widespread or at least not unique. All in all, however, even after the effort of putting together this book, I still find the Hull dialect fascinating and enjoyable. It is certainly has as many unique strings to its bow as any other of the major dialects around the country.

To the Hull people and their fascinating dialect – thank you.

BIBLIOGRAPHY & ACKNOWLEDGEMENTS:

Paul Kerswill (one of the country's leading sociolinguists, working at the University of Reading)
http://www.phon.ucl.ac.uk/home/dick/projects.htm

The Book of Words Tim Glynne-Jones 2008 Arcturus Publishing Ltd
London
ISBN: 978-1-84837-191-0

Talking for Britain Simon Elmes 2005 Penguin Books Ltd
ISBN: 0-140-51562-3

Hull's Fishing Heritage: Aspects of Life in the Hessle Road Fishing Community' Alec Gill 2003 Wharncliffe Books

Whisker, K. Merrison, A.J. and Swift, N. (2007) TH-fronting in Hull:
Investigating the Inland Revenue. York Working Papers in Linguistics
Series 2, Issue 8

Websites:

BBC Hull / Voices 2005
www.teachit.co.uk/armoore/lang/britishisles.htm

www.eastriding.gov.uk/corp-docs/forwardplanning/docs/lca/final/10000s/
Beverley.pdf
This is the East Riding of Yorkshire Landscape Character Assessment
www.peevish.co.uk/slang/s.htm

http://www.gracesguide.co.uk/wiki/Tan-Sad
This is Grace's guide – the best of British engineering 1750 – 1960s.

http://www.lylesgoldensyrup.com/faq.php

Boyes and Raynors Photos: Courtesy of Alec Gill.

INDIVIDUALS:

Quentin Budworth – *Artist and Musician.*

Joan & Brian Butler - *friends.*

Leanne Brown - *BBC Look North.*

David (Burnsy) Burns - *BBC Radio Humberside.*

Andy Comfort – *BBC Radio Humberside.*

Paul Dennis – *Publisher, Artist & Graphic Designer.*

Phil Haskins – *Hull Civic Society & organiser of the Heritage Open Days.*

Alan Kaye – *Author who contacted me with ideas and help.*

Rachel Kenington – *Belmont Taxis Ltd.*

Jo Makel – *BBC Look North.*

Vanessa McCoid – *friend & ex-colleague.*

Sylvia Rocke – *who rang me out of the blue with some help.*

Helen Scholefield – *BBC Radio Humberside.*

Nikki Swift – *York St John's University.*

Rose and Ron Turner – *my in-laws.*

Jayne and Antony Wilson – *friends.*

Angus Young – *Hull Daily Mail.*

Shane Rhodes – *Wrecking Ball Press.*

Oh! and especially to Lesley, Carolyn, Martin and Anita. Yes a special mention is required for my family and friends and their friends who have either talked to me or to each other on my behalf to identify words and phrases that I might add to my lists. Also, and with equal importance, those people who have listened to conversations and pointed things out that have been said or pronounced.

Grateful thanks also go to
Hull City Council Arts Unit for allowing
us to promote the book and give away 100 of them
in our "LUVULL EXPRESS!" promotion.
Part of the Humber Mouth Literature Festival.
·····2013·····

LUVULL.COM
Publications

www.luvull.com